P9-DCH-995

bliss to you

Copyright © 2008 by Dean Koontz

All rights reserved. No part of this book may be used or
reproduced in any manner whatsoever without the written
permission of the Publisher. Printed in the United States of
America. For information address Hyperion, 77 West 66th Street,
New York, New York 10023-6298.

Library of Congress Cataloging-in-Publication Data

Koontz, Dean R. (Dean Ray)
    Bliss to you : Trixie's guide to a happy life / Trixie Koontz,
as told to Dean R Koontz.
    p. cm.
ISBN 978-1-4013-2300-4
1. Dogs—Miscellanea. 2. Dogs—Pictorial works. I. Title.
SF426.2K634 2008
636.70022'2—dc22   2008026513

Hyperion books are available for special promotions, premiums, or
corporate training. For details contact Michael Rentas, Proprietary Markets,
Hyperion, 77 West 66th Street, 12th floor, New York, New York 10023,
or call 212-456-0133.

First Edition

10 9 8 7 6 5 4 3 2 1

bliss to you

BY TRIXIE KOONTZ, DOG
AS TOLD TO DEAN KOONTZ

NEW YORK

I, Trixie, who is dog,
dedicate this book to my human mom, Gerda,
whose quiet voice and kind eyes
always filled me with joy.

contents

Totos
trixie on the other side

BY DEAN KOONTZ

Our Trixie, a beautiful golden retriever with the tempera-
ment of an angel, who was a child to us, passed from this
world three months before her twelfth birthday, shortly after
2:00 on a Saturday afternoon. She resides now with many
other good dogs in the meadows at Rainbow Bridge, where
she waits for us to leave this world and join her.

For months after my wife, Gerda, and I lost our wonderful
girl, our grief was acute. In the weeks immediately after her
passing, when 2:00 Saturday afternoon approached, the
memory of her became so sharp that we could not bear to do
anything mundane. We walked together, hand in hand,
around these two and a half acres that Trixie had loved,
visiting all her favorite places.

Three weeks to the minute after Trixie died, as we were walking the larger lawn, a brilliant golden butterfly swooped down out of a pepper tree. This was no butterfly like we had ever seen before—or since. It was big, bigger than my hand, and a bright gold, not yellow. It flew around our heads three or four times, brushing our faces, our hair, as no butterfly, in our experience, had ever done before. Then it swooped back up past the pepper tree and vanished into the sky. Gerda, who is the most levelheaded person I have ever known, said at once, "Was that Trixie?" and without hesitation, I said, "Yeah. It was."

We didn't say another word about the experience until later, near bedtime, when we both commented on the incredible thickness of the butterfly's wings, which were too thick to have been aerodynamic. Gerda remembered them as being "almost edged in neon rope," and to me they had seemed to be like stained glass with a leaded edge. No landscaper who works here has ever before or since seen such a butterfly, nor have we; and it danced about our heads at the very minute that Trixie had died three weeks earlier.

Skeptics will wince, and I feel sorry for them. I will always believe that our girl wanted to let us know that the intensity of our grief was not appropriate, that she was all right. In sharing this story with friends, I have heard others who, after losing a beloved dog, had uncanny experiences quite differ-ent from ours but which also seemed to be intended to tell them that the spirit of their dog somehow lived on.

On my Website, Trixie's page routinely is one of the most visited features. With her photos and her writings, she won many fans of her own. I promised them that they would be hearing more from Trixie because, after all, her spirit is immortal. When Trixie posts messages and musings these days, they are labeled TOTOS, which is an acronym for Trixie on the Other Side.

And now, in your hands, you hold her third book. She published her first and second while she was alive, but channeled this one to me by way of my computer. Each evening, I would turn off the machine, and each morning I would find it on again, the screen bright with another chapter that had been sent from Rainbow Bridge.

Consequently, here is my furry daughter's third book, in which she offers dog wisdom that she hopes will bring more joy into her readers' lives. The author's royalties will be donated to Canine Companions for Independence, the won-derful organization that provides highly trained assistance dogs for people with disabilities.

what my book is about

BY TRIXIE KOONTZ

Bliss to you. Is me, Trixie Koontz, who was dog, is dog, always will be dog. Dog is very best thing to be. If you are dog, reading this, you know is true. If you are human reader—trust me.

I am dog, and dog can't lie.

Dog might tease stupid cat when shouldn't. Dog might tie sleeping cat to box-kite, cat wakes up two hundred feet above the earth, looks down, sees dog grinning and waving.

Dog might eat picnic frankfurters when no one looking. Dog might then eat potato salad. Dog might then eat apple pie. Dog might leave nothing for humans to eat except celery sticks.

Am not suggesting this behavior to your dog. Am just saying what naughty dogs might do. Not "bad" dogs. There are no bad dogs, only bad dog owners. That's the line naughty dogs find most successful in court, and is true.

Or left alone while rest of family goes out to dinner, naughty dog might pee on floor to make statement. Try it next time you want to make statement to spouse or children. Really works.

But dogs can't lie.

Dogs can't drive, either. Don't get me started. Is so unfair. Dogs are more responsible than average Hollywood starlet, and starlets all drive. Mostly drunk. Dogs drink only water. Maybe fruit juice. Not fermented fruit juice, either. In interest of public safety, law should allow good dogs to drive for Hollywood starlets.

I, Trixie, who am dog, wrote two other books. *Life is Good: Lessons in Joyful Living* and *Christmas is Good*. Never thought would write third. Is in Koontz Family blood—insane need to write. The other night, wanted to howl at moon. Instead, sat at computer and *wrote about* howling at moon. May need counseling.

Anyway, this book is about bliss—what it is and how you find it. Humans all want bliss but end up instead in jail or traffic court, or rehab, or broke in Las Vegas, or lost at sea, or gutting halibut in stinking hold of Alaskan fishing trawler and wondering—*How did I get here?*

All dogs know the secret of how to achieve bliss. And here on Other Side, in company of angels who toss tennis balls for us and give us belly rubs, I have learned even more about the subject.

I, Trixie, love humans. All good dogs do. Want humans to know true bliss without jail afterward. Road to bliss is paved with dog wisdom. I will show you the way to bliss. Follow me.

the first step to bliss:

Calm

The world is busy. Is scary. Is too much, always coming at you. Phone calls, text messages, emails, spam but not the tasty kind. Freeway traffic, road rage, crowded malls. Little kids who pull your tail, psycho cats with spinning eyes, spooky coyote packs howling in canyon at night.

To find bliss, must first step sideways out of all the busy-scary. Can't step forward or back, 'cause will still be in crazy rush.

I, Trixie, don't mean zone out like you do sometimes when boss is talking. Don't mean drop out, become hobo, develop body odor so strong it kills small birds.

No matter what kind of busy-scary you're trapped in, is always calm place very close. Mostly, life is raging river. (This is what dogs call metaphor.) So sometimes you need to swim to shore, sit awhile.

Your life might seem worse than raging river. Might seem like plunging elevator. Then you are long way from bliss. You need to press button marked emergency stop.

Sideways step, swim to shore, emergency stop button: all take you to same place. Place is called Quiet Heart.

Dogs live most of life in Quiet Heart.
Humans live mostly next door in Desperate Heart.
Now and then will do you good to live
in our zip code.

After step, swim, or button, you'll know you're
not in Quiet Heart if is loud music, jabbering
voices. Maybe you're in barroom. Only calm
in barroom is when you get blotto and pass out.

You don't want the kind of calm followed by
killer headache, vomiting, or seeing unauthorized
video of your SpongeBob SquarePants imitation
on YouTube. You need take *second* step sideways.

You're still not in Quiet Heart if in crowd. Pack of dogs can be calm, but not often pack of humans.

If TV is on, is not Quiet Heart. We don't have TV in Quiet Heart. Or radio. Or video games. Or phones or even one BlackBerry. No Internet.

When at last in Quiet Heart,
you'll observe a lot, think a little.

Here are some things you *won't* think about:
work, politics, movies, TV, celebrities, video
games, finances, UFOs, things you don't have
but want, things you have but don't want,
global warming, global cooling, flesh-eating virus.

When you live in Quiet Heart awhile,
is many feelings will come over you,
but one for sure not allowed. Anger.

You can't be angry at Republicans, Democrats, neighbor, friend, mother, father, not even if have reason to be angry. Cannot be angry even at crazy Aunt Edna when she knits paw booties and berets with ear holes, makes you wear them when she visits.

Calm is first step on road to bliss. Can't be calm if angry.

Humans are afraid of calm. Move, move, always move. Fill lives with dramas, big and small. Think, think, always thinking, but never the special thoughts that come with calm.

Only kind of thoughts that matter.

So find your Quiet Heart.

Banish all anger.

Be calm.

Even if rabbit comes out in open, nibbles grass,
and you want so bad to chase, you can't.

Not if in Quiet Heart.

If you want to pee, do it now.
We won't have time to pee again
till we find bliss and you embrace it.

the second step to bliss:

Beauty

The world is beautiful place.

Don't mean just big beautiful like starry sky.
Like Grand Canyon. Like Painted Desert.
Like crazy-huge beautiful ocean brings
all kinds smelly things to shore,
and you sniff, sniff, sniff,
and maybe eat one and then throw up.

Mean also *small* beautiful like shell of ladybug. Like color of carrots and shape of pears. Like moon all broken into shiny pieces on water. Like gorgeous black dog nose, pebble-textured and cold.

Mean even teeny-tiny beautiful like snowflake.
Like one drop water reflects world around it,
whole scene in one drop. Like the pattern of
crack lines and bubbles in piece of ice.
Like rising moon at bottom of human fingernail.

Dogs—like me, Trixie—are amazed by beauty of world. Amazed not just sometimes but 24/7. Butterflies! Songbirds! Roses! Cats! Even cats are beautiful! Psycho, scheming, sneaky, but beautiful!

World not perfect like once was. Not everything beautiful. Cow poop not beautiful. Dead rat not beautiful. Aunt Edna's six-toed feet not beautiful except maybe to Uncle Bud. But all those things smell really interesting, so beauty isn't everything.

Humans don't see beauty of the world 24/7. Sometimes not even 2/5. Is sad.

See sad, must do something. Why? Am dog. Want world as happy as dogs are happy. Only thing want as much as happy world is sausages.

To find true bliss, you must see beauty of natural world all around you. Beauty helps calm you. Bad day at work, you almost assaulted fellow worker with stapler. Spend evening in garden, star-gazing, cuddling puppy, will lose homicidal urge. Learn to see beauty of world 24/7 is must-do before you take next six steps to bliss.

To see beauty of world, you must really, really, really look. Not look *through*. Not look *at*. Must look *into*.

Most of time, you look at tree and see new car you want or problem at work. Not good. Is looking *through*, mind too busy to see.

Or you look at tree and see just tree. Is good to see just tree if driving car, so won't hit big old oak, have huge repair bill, be required to take breathalyzer test. But look at tree and see just tree is only looking *at*.

Look at tree, see strong roots vanish in earth, see texture of bark so intricate, limbs like vaulted ceiling in cathedral, green leaves that breathe, lacework of shadows and sunshine, see giver of shade on hot day, barrier to wind, shelter to birds, lumber to build homes. See the miracle that is tree. This is looking *into*.

Would you like cookie?

I would like cookie.

Life without cookie would be like...
No metaphor occurs to me.
Life without cookie unthinkable.

Get cookie, meet you back here ten seconds.

My cookie was good.

Your cookie looks better. See how I am really looking *into* your cookie? I see the miracle that is your cookie.

Humans eat so slow. Maybe is because your names are not on your dishes, so you're never sure it's your food, is okay to eat.

While I wait for you to slow eat,
will get second cookie. Six seconds.

Hello again. Am back, me, Trixie Koontz, dog and author and happy cookie-eater.

Took extra twenty-two seconds to contemplate line I read in Proust last night. Still makes no sense. Proust is no Dr. Seuss.

Okay. Onward to bliss.

Why is so hard for humans learn to look *into* things, see beauty everywhere?

One reason: desire. Humans mostly think about what they want next. Always thinking what is wanted next, you live in future, never in *now*. Can't see beauty of world, which is now, if you are full of desire for what you want next Tuesday.

Dogs never know what comes next. Always surprised. Might be skin infection, might be entire meatloaf dropped on floor. No point in dog having desire because dogs can't control future.

Want to know secret? You can't control future, either. Here it comes, skin infection or meatloaf.

Is rhythm of life: meatloaf, skin infection, bag of potato chips left open on low table, meteor through roof. Good thing about life is, there's always lots more meatloaf than meteors.

Another same-but-different reason humans find so hard to look into things: pleasure. Many humans live for pleasure.

Nothing wrong with pleasure. Dogs also like pleasure. My cookies were pleasure. Your better cookie was probably ecstasy.

So desire distracts from now, where life is lived. And pleasure without context leads to life without meaning.

You say "context" and "meaning" are concepts too big for dog mind. You are so wrong. Dog can chase ball, brood on mysteries of universe at same time. You don't know this because you only look *at* dogs.

Is okay you only look *at* dogs. Are so cute, is hard to see past surface. But dogs are like the sea—sparkle of sunlight on surface but whole world below. Much in life is that way.

Except cats. Cats are cute. But what you see is what you get.

So we were talking about pleasure.
You must see deep beauty of world, of life,
to get full enjoyment from pleasure.
Pleasure without beauty is just empty thrill.

Like you bite open plastic jar of peanut butter,
eat entire contents. Delicious now. But making
pig of self is not beautiful. So, later feel shame.
And have big intestinal-tract distress.

Beauty of the world, of life, puts pleasure in context 'cause beauty is better than pleasure. Pleasure passes, beauty endures (dog wisdom). Beauty of world, of life, is gift. Pleasure taken with awareness of gift is thank-you, and we all feel good saying thank you.

Already, more dog wisdom: beauty of world includes human face. Dogs love every human face. Humans love only some. Is no ugly face. Only different beauty. Human who never gives you cookie can still be beautiful.

Take fourteen seconds, think about that.

Okay. Two steps. One, be calm.
Two, see the world in all its beauty.

You have completed Step Two. Good human.

I would lick your face if you were here.

You're welcome.

the third step to bliss:
Fun

The world is fun. Meadows to run.
Ponds to swim. Hills, valleys, shores
to explore. A bajillion things to smell.
So much to learn, to see. Cats to chase.

Warning: can't achieve bliss if catch cat.
Cats are only for chasing. Catch cat,
get lacerated nose, go to vet, get cuts
sewn shut, needle in butt, and everybody
laughing, especially cat.

The world is a gift to make you happy.

You don't think of it as gift because didn't come wrapped in bright paper with bow. Didn't have gift tag on with message: *Dear Loretta, Here is your world. Have a happy life. Love, God.*

Also hard to think world is gift because is so extravagant. Is like you invite someone to dinner, they bring you hostess gift of two matched Mercedes.

But world is great gift. Dogs know this. We are always happy. Except when we see how humans sometimes refuse happiness. Then we are sad for you.

Is true: *dogs know*. Some say "dogs rule." Is not true. If dogs ruled, you'd pay taxes with frankfurters. But dogs *know*.

Happiness is a choice. You can choose happy or unhappy, no matter what happens. No one else can make you happy. Must make happy yourself.

Think about this. (Don't panic. Is not Proust you must think about. Is not even Dr. Seuss.) Sun is 330,000 times bigger than Earth, is seething mass of thermonuclear reactions. Sometimes sun cools down teeny bit, Earth has ice age. Sometimes sun heats up teeny bit, Earth gets way hotter. Someday sun might heat up smidgin more than teeny bit, incinerate Earth instantly. Also, planet's magnetic pole could shift, destroy civilization in one day.

So why be glum about cooking with trans-fatty acids?

Humans and dogs so small. Universe so big, even bigger than biggest Wal-Mart, full of things that go boom and bang. Yet we thrive.

Be happy we thrive. Embrace fun, not gloom.

Now I will get cookie before magnetic pole shifts. Be back in twenty-one seconds.

Was excellent cookie. Worthy of cover story for *Gourmet* magazine. Living on edge of planetary disaster made cookie taste even better.

Laughter is tranquilizer without side effects. Best laughter is laughter at self. My human dad, who is author, has said life is parade of fools and he is at front of parade with a baton.

If can laugh at self, are guaranteed more fun in life.

Some truths about fun:

You don't need yacht to have fun. Rowboat
will do. And just because other guy has yacht,
doesn't make rowboat less fun.

Box of lemon-custard doughnuts is still good
thing even if guy next door has four boxes.

Excuse me. Am going next door.
Be back in forty seconds or half hour.

No doughnuts next door. I, Trixie Koontz,
am always eager to experience singular glory
of baked goods. Knew doughnuts were
hypothetical, yet had to be sure.

Optimism is required for fun.

Sometimes hypothetical doughnuts turn out to be real. You would never find them if didn't look.

Can be optimistic only if you limit worry
to things you can change. Can't change path
of massive asteroid hurtling toward Earth.
Can't change sun getting hotter or cooler.
Can't avoid flesh-eating bacteria just by moving,
leaving no forwarding address.

If expect bad to happen, spend all life in gloom,
waiting. And sometimes, expecting bad things
is like magnet: bad things are drawn toward you.

Optimism is like mental cookie.
Cookie nourishes tummy.
Optimism nourishes heart.

Thomas Jefferson said life mostly sunshine.
Hitler said life mostly suffering. Freud said
life meaningless.

You *know* whose dog had more fun.

time out for some
dog wisdom

You, who are reader, have taken three steps toward bliss. Need to rest briefly. Need to meditate. Here are dog wisdoms maybe worth meditating about.

Don't bite at buzzing bee.
Get stung. Face swells.
Look like pig with fur.

Encourage beer drinking
at summer picnics.
Drunks drop more food.

Never judge a person
by his appearance.
Judge him by his smell.

If Dad catches you
driving convertible,
claim cat made you do it
at gunpoint.

When you stop to smell roses,
be careful not to inhale bee.

If every day is first day
of your life, maybe you are
being perpetually infantile.

When throwing party,
remember cats can't hold
their liquor.

Eat grass, throw up.
Doesn't sound like fun,
but is.

Love and sausage are alike.
Can never have enough
of either.

Dogs love to make fools
of themselves. Join in.
We won't tell anybody.

If humans had fur like dogs,
would be no garment industry.

A puppy is the only love
that money can buy.

Mailman does not come
to house **to kill us all**.
Comes to house to **torture**
and then kill.

Paws are better than hands.
Paws cannot forge signatures,
cannot point fingers of blame,
cannot pull gun trigger,
cannot make obscene gestures,
cannot pick pockets.

Moon probably not made of cheese. But if is one chance in ten million is made of cheese, we must triple annual NASA budget.

Jack Sprat could eat no fat.
His wife could eat no lean.
More for the dog.

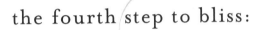

the fourth step to bliss:

Meaning

Is your world. You belong here. No less
or more than anyone, you belong. You are
not Martian. You are Earthling. *Bienvenu!*
Come in! Make yourself at home! Light and
rest your saddle! Is no welcome basket
of free goodies and half-off coupons,
but is nevertheless super-nice planet.

Is still necessary you bathe, brush teeth, learn manners, and don't pick nose in public. Belonging comes with as many responsibilities as rights.

Picking nose *in private* is your right, but comes with serious responsibility to wash hands after.

One responsibility is discover reason why you are here.

Is no politician can give your life meaning. Seek meaning from politician is like buy package bologna with hope will find messages from God hidden between slices.

No Internet site can tell you. No single book. No CD with title like "30 Days to Wealth, Fame, and World Domination."

Each has to find own way. Read, inquire, think, pray.

Everyone has own reason for being here,
unique to him or her. Like your fingerprint
is unique. Like your DNA is unique.

Like your smell is unique, so dog could
track you through swampy Everglades,
through Miami, all the way to Key West,
arrest you for crime, assuming you are criminal
and assuming dog has police authority.

Some humans don't believe each person
is here for a reason. They say are here
only to breed, eat, die.

Be careful of humans who say such stuff.
Is philosophy of praying mantis that breeds
with mate then eats mate alive on same date.

You do not want eaten alive on date. Reason you are here might be mystery, but is not to be dinner.

When using Internet dating service, ask what happened to applicant's previous date. If answer is "was eaten alive," you have not found spouse of your dreams.

Here is what real meaning is like.
Maybe you're meant to give kindness
to one special child. Child grows up,
is healer or wise leader. Then your purpose
was as big as any king's, maybe bigger.

Because you do something well, doesn't mean is your life purpose. Maybe you are whiz at poker. Have fun. Make money. But poker can't give meaning to life.

Dogs play poker so good, have inspired renowned paintings of canine card games. Lost Rembrandts, stolen from Louvre in World War II, show late-Renaissance dogs enjoying early version of five-card stud.

But dogs' purpose is not card games. Or even tennis balls. Dogs' purpose is give love, teach loyalty, teach courage, show humans how to have fun.

Your purpose might be to die to save others or to protect their rights, meaning rights way more important than right to pick nose in private. Humans die for others every day.

Is our responsibility to honor them.
They are the best of humanity.

Of all animals, only dogs die to save human life. Never saw cow jump into lake to tow drowning boy to shore. Never saw hamster chase off armed burglar. Only dog. Is one reason man and dog have bond. We are guardians of each other. We share a destiny.

Is many traits we share, too. Humans and dogs are only creatures that love play throughout life. Both crave affection. Value loyalty. See mystery in world. Get excited by Frisbee.

Trixie, me, knew fry cook who liked Frisbee. (This is what authors call "smooth transitional sentence." Just keep reading.)

Maybe you are on Earth to be fry cook. Don't think is small destiny. Making food that comforts is great thing.

Here at Rainbow Bridge, where animal companions wait for our beloved humans to arrive, we smell food in Heaven. Is lots of great fry cooks over there.

Can't find really good transitional sentence, so am just moving on:

Maybe you are on Earth to inspire others. Like teachers and ministers do. Like a Down's syndrome child inspires by overcoming limitations with good heart, sweet smile.

So how to find your purpose?

First, ask self what you enjoy doing most. If answer is not criminal activity, might be your purpose.

If answer is "eat, drink, sleep, party, shop," you do not understand question. *Purpose* means what you contribute. Looking cool is not contribution.

Ask self what people you admire most.
Maybe what you admire them doing is what
you are meant to do.

Maybe your purpose is raise good children.
World needs good children. Has enough bullies.

Maybe your purpose is rescue abused abandoned dogs, give homes. Then you are saint. In Heaven, angels will give you dishes with your name on, so you can be sure food is yours, eat fast and carefree.

No purpose is too small if it makes life better for others. A good nurse relieves more pain than any movie star.

Find your true purpose, you will find your bliss.

the fifth step to bliss:
Others

Is famous human saying: no man is an island. For long time I, Trixie, who is reasonably perceptive and analytic dog, thought saying was stupid. What means—no man is an island? No man is continent, either. No man is ocean. No man is square block of Cleveland.

Met man who *smelled* like nine square blocks of Cleveland, distilled into one person, but is another story. Is not appealing story, so probably will never write it. Is rule of thumb in writing game: if story requires many long descriptions of smells so vile will give reader nausea, is not likely to find publisher.

I, Trixie, who has no thumbs, obey rule anyway. Is because dogs like to live by rules as long as rules are fair. Guidelines give comfort.

Anyway, one day realized "No man is an island" means people need people, said in just five words when Ms. Barbra Streisand needed whole song. Since dogs need people, too, enlightenment came like delicious strip of bacon.

Would prefer real bacon,
but will settle for enlightenment.

To achieve bliss, must live in Quiet Heart
but must also have *open* heart.
Is hard to find bliss when lonely.

Am not talking romance.
Am not Danielle Steele, folks.

If was talking romance, would have mentioned
Beatles' song "All You Need Is Love" instead
of Ms. Barbra's song. Would have been cliché,
but dogs do not fear clichés, will chase cars
and pee on fire plugs, not be embarrassed.

When say "others," am not even talking friends. Friends can be good. You need good friends.

But friends also can be people have bad influence, people you pass out drunk with. Can be people you rob banks with. Dracula and Frankenstein monster were friends sometimes in old movies, but was not healthy life-affirming relationship.

Am talking people who, in their lives,
you make really good difference. Like people
have no food at Christmas, you give them turkeys.

(Giving turkeys to dogs also counts.)

Or senior citizen is homebound, you do errands
for her. Or disabled neighbor can't mow lawn,
you mow it.

Trixie, who is me, was one time assistance dog
to person with disability. Was trained by Canine
Companions for Independence. Many, many
people volunteer thousands hours to CCI
each year.

Is what meant when titled Fifth Step "Others."
Living for others as much as for self is BIG step
toward bliss. Living for others, can't be bored.
Living for others, have no time to feel sorry for self.
Living for others is best answer to: why am I here,
what does life mean, does anybody care,
do I matter?

Living for others won't answer every question. Like: why did chicken cross the road? Why do firemen wear red suspenders? Which came first, chicken or egg?

Those are cosmic questions God answers only when we die. No reasonable human would expect answers to cosmic questions in book written by dog, so don't send me email wanting money back.

Besides no-man-is-island thing, another human saying used to seem dumb to me is: you want to have your cake and eat it, too.

Still seems dumb. If eat cake, you still do have it. Cake is now part of you. I am 3% cake, 3% apple slices and other fruit, 7% chicken, 5% beef, 2% fish, 2% ham, 2% cheese, 1% rice cakes with strawberry jam, 2% peanut butter, 50% kibble, 1% corn and potato chips, 22% miscellaneous.

Only way can *not* have cake and eat it too is if eat cake and then throw it up. Who wants that?

Here is another dumb saying: it is what it is. No kidding. If it *isn't* what it is, then what would it be? And if it is what it *isn't*, what the hell is going on here?

Sorry about foul language. Is not like me. But even dogs sometimes get annoyed.

Here is really dumb saying: be careful what you wish for. Whoa, thanks for warning! Almost wished lightning would strike my butt. Close one. Almost wished would be attacked by pack of rabid cats. What was I thinking?

Some human sayings not dumb,
just painfully obvious. Like: what goes up
must come down. *Duh.* Or: what goes around
comes around. Double *duh.* Or: whatever will be
will be. Unless it isn't what it is.

Those sayings have nothing to do with Fifth Step to Bliss. Am just venting.

Writing book is stressful. Must take time to return to Quiet Heart. Give me fifty seconds.

Only needed seven. Almost fell asleep.

Anyway, Fifth Step is to live for others. This you *can* learn from dogs. Dogs live for people. Why you think our tails are most always wagging?

the sixth step to bliss:
Humility

I, Trixie, who is philosophical dog, been thinking which came first—dog or kibble? Dog or blue poop-pickup bags? Dog or plush toys with squeaker inside? Dog or cookie?

Have decided kibble, blue bags, squeaky toys, and cookies all came first because God wanted everything dogs need to be here before dogs arrived.

Means people also came before dogs because dogs need people to tell us how cute we are. So dogs were last things put on earth— peak of Creation.

Peak of creation!
Dogs, dogs, dogs!

Many proofs dogs are peak of Creation.
Is no dog equivalent of Paris Hilton.
Is no dog would wear plaids, stripes together.
No dog ever tied human to post, left alone
in backyard. No dog ever got drunk,
woke up next morning in bed with strange cat.

Dogs rule! Peak of creation!
Dogs, dogs, dogs!

Foregoing text is example of what is not humility.

Was embarrassing to write. If didn't have fur, my blushing would be obvious.

Humility is important step to bliss.

Opposite of humility—big ego, arrogance.

Nobody likes big-ego arrogant humans.
Arrogant humans have no true friends,
only fake friends. Like Count Dracula
and Frankenstein's monster were not
really friends. (See Step Five.)

Arrogant people can't find purpose. Maybe can find money, fame, power— but not purpose with meaning. Because are too busy loving themselves.

Time is hard on arrogant people. Even arrogant people are small compared to universe. Time will teach them how small.

St. Francis said, "Where there is patience and humility, there is neither anger nor vexation."

Vexation means worry, confusion, torment.
Had to look up in human dictionary.
Could not find in dog dictionary.

St. Francis was wise. He said console
others instead of seeking to be consoled,
love others instead of seeking to be loved,
understand instead of seeking to be understood.
He said give dogs all the cookies they want.

Last one is not true. Am ashamed,
trying to use St. Francis to scam treat.

Here's something dogs like to do.
Lie on lawn, on back, stare at stars.
Think how big is universe, how small is me.
Think how long is time, how short is life here.

Makes you feel good because you realize
cannot change the world, only brighten corner
where you are.

Fame means nothing. Time erases fame.

Great power doesn't last. Time erases the powerful.

Your anger dies with you.

What love you give lives on.

Cynic will sneer at this truth. Time erases cynics.

You have as much love to give as any king or movie star. If humble, you have *more* to give than king or movie star.

time out for some

wisdom
about dogs

Here is not wisdom *from* dog, me, Trixie. Here is wisdom *about* dogs, said by people. My comments follow after each. Is much to learn here.

IF YOU PICK UP A STARVING DOG
AND MAKE HIM PROSPEROUS,
HE WILL NOT BITE YOU.
THIS IS THE PRINCIPAL DIFFERENCE
BETWEEN A DOG AND A MAN.

~Mark Twain

Is perfect spot for cat joke. In spirit of charity,
will restrain self.

I LOVE A DOG. HE DOES NOTHING
FOR POLITICAL REASONS.

~**Will Rogers**

And dog makes no promises it can't keep,
kisses only babies it loves.

THERE IS NO FAITH WHICH HAS NEVER
YET BEEN BROKEN EXCEPT THAT OF
A TRULY FAITHFUL DOG.

~Konrad Lorenz

And look how happy dogs are. Means keeping
vows make you happier than breaking them.

A DOG IS THE ONLY THING ON EARTH
THAT LOVES YOU MORE THAN
HE LOVES HIMSELF.

~Josh Billings

Dogs give unconditional love so you will be
teensy bit prepared for God's love when you die
and meet Him. Otherwise, God's love would
knock you flat.

THE DOG HAS SELDOM BEEN SUCCESSFUL
IN PULLING MAN UP TO ITS LEVEL OF SAGACITY,
BUT MAN HAS FREQUENTLY DRAGGED THE DOG
DOWN TO HIS.

~James Thurber

Trying to change that with my book. But am only
dog. Still easily misled with treats or tennis ball.

DOGS LOVE COMPANY. THEY PUT IT FIRST
ON THEIR SHORT LIST OF NEEDS.

~J. R. Ackerley

After die, will be waiting for you at Rainbow Bridge.
There, will be enough alone to last forever. Here and
in Heaven, let's have fun together.

YOU THINK DOGS WILL NOT BE IN HEAVEN.
I TELL YOU, THEY WILL BE THERE
LONG BEFORE ANY OF US.

~Robert Louis Stevenson

And will start putting in good word for you
from moment we arrive there.

THE DOG WAS CREATED
ESPECIALLY FOR CHILDREN.
HE IS THE GOD OF FROLIC.

~Henry Ward Beecher

If you let us, in your old age, we'll make you child again. Play and laughter deny time its power.

EXCAVATORS DIGGING THROUGH THE VOLCANIC ASH
THAT BURIED THE RUINS OF POMPEII IN A.D. 79
DISCOVERED A DOG LYING ACROSS A CHILD
[TRYING TO PROTECT IT]. THE DOG, WHOSE NAME
WAS DELTA, WORE A COLLAR THAT TOLD
HOW HE HAD SAVED THE LIFE OF HIS OWNER,
SEVERINUS, THREE TIMES.

~John Richard Stevens

Is nothing to make you feel better than knowing
you gave all you could.

PEOPLE HAVE A HARD TIME ACHIEVING HAPPINESS
IN THEIR LIVES. THEY TEND TO GET WRAPPED UP
IN THEIR OWN LITTLE WORLD. PEOPLE GET
CONFUSED BECAUSE THEY DO NOT KNOW
WHAT THEY NEED OR WANT, AND THEN
DEPRESSION SETS IN. DOGS DO NOT HAVE
THIS PROBLEM. THEY KNOW EXACTLY WHAT
MAKES THEM HAPPY—DOING SOMETHING
FOR SOMEONE. THEY WILL DO EVERYTHING
THEY CAN THINK OF TO PLEASE THEIR HUMAN
COMPANIONS, AND ANY SIGNS THAT THEY
HAVE BEEN SUCCESSFUL MAKE THEM VERY HAPPY.

~John Richard Stevens

Live for self is boring. Every day is same wants,
needs, desires. Live for others, is always variety,
surprise, delight.

the seventh step to bliss:
Loss

Accepting loss. Losses that have happened, losses to come. Cannot find bliss until can accept loss.

Might be hardest of eight steps to understand. Is loss that hurts more than anything. Loss of spouse or child or parent. Loss of beloved pet. Hurts worse than physical pain.

Why death? Why pain?

Remember, am just dog, me, Trixie, but here's
what I was told by my dog mom, who was
wiser than me.

At first, world did not have pain or death.
Animals lived in peace forever—humans, too.
We all hung out at Starbucks, went to vegetarian
restaurants, danced the conga—or maybe
I'm confused about that part. Anyway,
no pain, no death, peace forever.

Humans were given free will. Means they were not animals but one step below angels. Humans, only humans, were so free they could do whatever they wanted—obey natural laws or not.

Some chose not. By choosing bad, they opened door to evil, brought pain and death into world.

Am very glad wasn't dog made bad choice. We get blamed every new spot on carpet whether was us or not. Can imagine scolding we'd get if ruined entire world.

So then some humans fell into envy, greed, jealousy, and worse. No need to go there. You know what is worse. World became violent place.

Consider all that next time before say, "Bad dog."

But bringing death and pain into world, humans also brought chance for redemption. Loss is hardest thing but also is teacher most difficult to ignore.

If you never knew pain or loss, never grief, how would you learn compassion? Empathy for others comes from understanding their suffering. Without experience of loss, of pain, humans would be monsters caring only about their own pleasure.

Grief teaches humility, teaches compassion.

Am only dog, me, Trixie Koontz, so would like to quote from my human dad's book, *ODD HOURS*, on subject. He's human but dog, too, in his way, so can say maybe better than me, but with some canine wisdom. Just hope he doesn't charge me fee for quote:

Grief can destroy you—or focus you.

You can decide a relationship was all for nothing if it had to end in death, and you alone.

Or you can realize that every moment of it had more meaning than you dared to recognize at the time, so much meaning it scared you, so you just lived, just took for granted the love and laughter of each day, and didn't allow yourself to consider the sacredness of it.

But when it's over and you're alone,
you begin to see it wasn't just a movie
and a dinner together, not just watching
sunsets together, not just scrubbing a floor
or washing dishes together or worrying
over a high electric bill. Instead, it was
everything, it was the why of life,
every event and precious moment of it.

*The answer to the mystery of existence
is the love you shared sometimes so imperfectly,
and when the loss wakes you to the deeper
beauty of it, to the sanctity of it, you can't
get off your knees for a long time; you're driven
to your knees not by the weight of the loss
but by gratitude for what preceded the loss.*

*And the ache is always there, but one day
not the emptiness, because to nurture
the emptiness, to take solace in it,
is to disrespect the gift of life.*

Is me again, Trixie Koontz, dog.

When you accept loss and understand
why must happen, cannot be bitter.
Can be depressed only short while.

Humans love all things that cannot last.
Is good to love what does not last—if also love,
even more, what does last.

Love calm that leads to Quiet Heart because
next life will all be lived with a quiet heart.

Love beauty of the world because
is preview of the beauty of eternity.

Love fun and laughter because
you were made for joy.

Love—and live for—others because, like you, they are here for reason, and like you, they outlast the world. When abandoned or abused dog is saved by dog-rescue group, rescuers place it in what is called a "forever home." Love others because they will one day share your forever home, maybe even Aunt Edna with six-toed feet.

Love humility in others, not fame.
Find humility in self but take no pride in it.

So here we come to Step Eight, last step to bliss.
Now you will discover why achieving bliss
is kind of like shedding fur.

the eighth step to bliss:
Gratitude

Cookies! Sausage! Apples!
Cake! Kibble! Chicken! Lamb!
Rice! Peaches! Mashed taters!
Carrots! Ice cream! Halibut!
Did I say kibble? **Kibble!!!**
Peanut butter!!!!!!!!

Is tendency of dog authors to overuse exclamation point. Is not result of poor schooling, but more genetic propensity related to joyful enthusiastic nature.

To avoid snarky remarks from book critics, have tried not to overuse exclamation point throughout. But when come to chapter on gratitude, cannot help self!

Cats never overuse exclamation point, will give them that. Not many cat authors write books. They write haiku, so have more time to lie around, sleep in sunshine. Am not claiming cats are lazy. They just have less to say.

Sunshine! Sunrise! Sunset! Rain! Walk in rain, fur wet, smell so good! Snow! Wind, wind, wind of a million smells!!!

When every day heart swells with gratitude
for all gifts of life, you are on brink of bliss.

To know such deep constant gratitude,
you had to shed so much.

Dogs know about shedding—except fancy breeds that have hair, not fur. Not their fault. Just their nature. Not their fault either if humans shave dog's hair in funny shapes and decorate with ribbons. Is same species—human—that opened door to evil and ruined world. Making dog look ridiculous is no big deal by comparison. Humans usually mean well, just don't always think things through.

To approach bliss, you had to shed anxiety and desperation that prevent calm, had to find Quiet Heart.

Very good. Sit. Stay. Enjoy.

To approach bliss, you had to shed blinders on your eyes that kept you from seeing beauty everywhere in world.

Am so proud of you. You have become human I could take anywhere.

To approach bliss, you had to realize
world is gift, is fun, happiness is your choice.
You had to shed gloom and tendency
to worry about things you can't control.

Give yourself cookie. You deserve.

To approach bliss, you had to shed doubt and see that life has meaning, you are here for a purpose. This is hard step for many— to admit you *matter,* that everything does.

I would give you tummy rub if you were here.

To approach bliss, you had to shed idea
that life is about you first, had to realize
life is about others.

Therefore you have overcome tendency
to think like cat.

To approach bliss, you had to shed pride,
had to shed idea that fame and power
are important. Had to see beauty of humility.

To approach bliss, you had to shed bitterness
that loss can inspire. Loss hurts because
what came before it was so sweet.

Be grateful for the sweet.

Be grateful for the lessons of loss that come to a humble heart, for others in your life who help you live with loss, for meaning those others bring to your life, for laughter you share with them, for beauty of world that allows us to laugh, and for quiet heart that makes it possible to see beauty.

Running in meadows! Swimming in lake! Chasing ball! Tug toys! Squeaky toys! The loving hand! The scratch behind ears! Cool water for thirst! Kitchens and all their smells! Visitors come to play! The human voice and the gentle word! Ears to hear with! Eyes to see! Tongue to taste! A heart big enough to hold it all—the wonder, the mystery, the beauty!

Oh, the grace.

Bliss to you. From me, Trixie Koontz, who is dog. Bliss to you forever.

CANINE COMPANIONS
FOR INDEPENDENCE

ALL AUTHOR PROCEEDS FROM THIS BOOK ARE DONATED
TO CANINE COMPANIONS FOR INDEPENDENCE.